How to use this devotional

Each day offers a reflection for the day, a verse and an
opportunity to dive deeper into the reading for the day.

Each day also offers space to write your conversations
with God and a prayer to help you grow closer to God.

Record your prayer requests and when God is answering
your prayers.

We would love to hear how you are learning to trust God.
Send us an email so we can celebrate with you the prayers
God has answered.

Joan Murray Ministries &
Seeds Of Hope Worldwide Missions
P.O. Box 5073
Katy, TX 77491
281-398-2501

Email: JMMContactus@gmail.com
www.JoanMurrayMinistries.org
Email: Contactus@seedsofhopemissions.org
www.Seedsofhopeworldwidemissions.org

Changing Lives Through the Power
and Truth of God's Word.

Daily Devotional

DATE: _____

REFLECTION OF THE DAY

You may find yourself disconnected from God and His perfect plan for your life, but you can return to Him today. God created man to have connection and fellowship with Him. This connection was to ensure our success. The enemy is determined to cause disconnection between you and God, and it is your responsibility to withstand Satan and overcome him. Examine the areas of your life that may have caused you to become estranged from the heart of God. Make a decision today to reestablish the connection by plugging into your Source of power—God.

VERSES OF THE DAY

John 10:10 – "The thief cometh not, but for to steal, and to kill, and to destroy: I am come that they might have life, and that they might have it more abundantly."

1 Peter 5:8 – "Be sober, be vigilant; because your adversary the devil, as a roaring lion, walketh about, seeking whom he may devour:"

HEART CHECK QUESTIONS:

1. Am I experiencing a disconnection from God?

2. When did I feel this disconnection?

3. How can I reconnect to the heart of God?

Connecting To The Heart Of God:

What steps can I take to deepen my relationship with Him?

Notes:

Prayer:

Father, I feel disconnected from Your heart. Show me how to reconnect to You and the great plans for my future. John 10:10 tells me the thief has robbed me with the intention to destroy me, but I have life in You, in Jesus' name. Amen!

DATE: _____

REFLECTION OF THE DAY

Adam and Eve experienced disconnection from God because they had a heart issue. Instead of longing after God, they longed after something else. We also lose our connection with God when we have issues in our hearts that we do not allow God to process or to deal with. These issues affect our relationship and fellowship with God and cause us to not fully understand that whatever affects our hearts will eventually affect our entire life. As you look back over your life, can you see where you got off track?

VERSES OF THE DAY

Psalms 139:23-24 - "Search me, O God, and know my heart: try me, and know my thoughts: And see if there be any wicked way in me, and lead me in the way everlasting."

Romans 8:7 – "Because the carnal mind is enmity against God: for it is not subject to the law of God, neither indeed can be."

HEART CHECK QUESTIONS:

1. What is the greatest longing of my heart?

2. What heart issues are affecting my life?

3. Identify how and why I lost my connection with God?

Connecting To The Heart Of God:

What steps can I take to deepen my relationship with Him?

Notes:

Prayer:

Father, I am asking You to search my heart and know my anxious thoughts. Help me to align my thoughts and life with You based on Psalm 139:23-24. Help me to deepen my connection with You, in Jesus' name. Amen!

Daily Devotional

DATE: _____

REFLECTION OF THE DAY

Just like Eve, we get so focused on the things we want we never see the danger signs. All we see is a light that beckons us. Isn't it interesting how the enemy can make things seem so appealing to our senses? We encounter problems when our heart longs after the wrong things. The right desires that should motivate us toward right choices are often hidden, and what we do not want to do are the things that keep resurfacing.

VERSES OF THE DAY

Mark 14:38 – "Watch ye and pray, lest ye enter into temptation. The spirit truly is ready, but the flesh is weak."

Proverbs 14:16 – "A wise man feareth, and departeth from evil: but the fool rageth, and is confident.

HEART CHECK QUESTIONS:

1. What danger signs am I overlooking in my life?

2. What is the enemy using to beckon me away from God's plan for my life?

3. What wrong desires are harassing me?

Connecting To The Heart Of God:

What steps can I take to deepen my relationship with Him?

<u>Notes:</u>

Prayer:

Father, please help me to not be enticed by the enemy. Help me to be wise in the decisions I make. Teach me how to watch and pray as I am told in Mark 14:38. Help me to have a willing heart to follow You, in Jesus' name. Amen!

Daily Devotional

DATE: _____

REFLECTION OF THE DAY

As you wrestle with unwholesome thoughts, remember these things are designed to keep you from bearing the right fruit in your life. Make the decision to neither give up nor submit to them. Your struggles are against the demonic influences that are all around you. The enemy went directly into Eve's presence to entice her away from God's plans. Today, he whispers in our ears and tells us the temptation we surrender to will not harm us. He wants you to believe there is nothing wrong with the unwholesome desires you feel. Ask yourself, "Is this God's best for me?"

VERSES OF THE DAY

James 4:17 – "Therefore to him that knoweth to do good, and doeth it not, to him it is sin."

James 4:7 – "Submit yourselves therefore to God. Resist the devil, and he will flee from you."

HEART CHECK QUESTIONS:

1. What am I wrestling with?

2. What fruit am I bearing each day?

3. Who is influencing my choices?

Connecting To The Heart Of God:

What steps can I take to deepen my relationship with Him?

Notes:

Prayer:

Father, help me to overcome all the unwholesome thoughts that are clouding my mind. I know that James 4:7 tells me to resist the devil and he will flee from me. Help me to fight the enemy and to be victorious, in Jesus' name. Amen!

Daily Devotional

DATE: _____

REFLECTION OF THE DAY

The Bible says out of our hearts flow the issues of life. What issues are you having? They are coming from a heart that does not have the right ingredients to produce the right results. Are you having an issue with your flesh? Are you having an issue with unstable emotions? Are you having an issue with unwholesome desires? Check what you are allowing to penetrate your heart because whatever you allow will birth these desires and bear the wrong fruit in your life. No one can securely guard your heart but you together with the Holy Spirit, and you have to allow Him access to do so.

VERSES OF THE DAY

Luke 6:45 – "A good man out of the good treasure of his heart bringeth forth that which is good; and an evil man out of the evil treasure of his heart bringeth forth that which is evil: for of the abundance of the heart his mouth speaketh.."

Hebrews 4:12 – "For the word of God is quick, and powerful, and sharper than any twoedged sword, piercing even to the dividing asunder of soul and spirit, and of the joints and marrow, and is a discerner of the thoughts and intents of the heart."

HEART CHECK QUESTIONS:

1. What issues are eroding my heart?

2. How can I overcome these heart issues?

3. How do I produce good fruit?

Connecting To The Heart Of God:

What steps can I take to deepen my relationship with Him?

Notes:

Prayer:

Jesus, help me as I face the hard issues in my life. Forgive me for allowing the devil to fill my heart with bad fruit. I desire my heart to be fill with Your truth. I need my heart to reflect the love and forgiveness You have poured into me. I desire a heart that produces good fruit, in Jesus' name. Amen!

Daily Devotional

DATE: _____

The issues of the heart are about how intensely you and I love God. Is our love for God intense enough we are willing to fight and overcome wrong desires in order to stay in close communion with Him? God has much to say about our hearts. When you have good stored in your heart, you will live a productive life that bears good results. To store good in your heart, you make a conscious decision to do what is right no matter how you feel or how enticing the temptations may be. Doing what is right is not a decision you make only one time; it is a decision you must make daily.

VERSES OF THE DAY

Proverbs 4:23 - "Keep thy heart with all diligence; for out of it are the issues of life."

Psalm 51:10 – "Create in me a clean heart, O God, and renew a right spirit within me."

HEART CHECK QUESTIONS:

1. Have I ever felt a deep love for God? What did I experience?

2. How can I guard my heart?

3. How do I keep my heart clean?

Connecting To The Heart Of God:

What steps can I take to deepen my relationship with Him?

Notes:

Prayer:

Father, Psalm 51 says to create in me a clean heart and renew a right spirit in me. I desire to develop a deeper love relationship with You; please show me how to love You like Jesus loves You, in Jesus' name. Amen!

Daily Devotional

DATE: _____

REFLECTION OF THE DAY

What do you think God's greatest treasure is? When God looks at His treasure, He sees you! You are His finest masterpiece. Jesus left His splendor, majesty, and worship to die for you because you are God's treasure. God has poured His excellence and power into you so you may understand He is the one who empowers you for greatness. Allow your greatest treasure to be Him. Let Him become the greatest issue of your heart so He can flow out of you to impact the hearts and lives of the people around you. Give God full access to your heart and life and watch as He reveals His treasure (you) to the world.

VERSES OF THE DAY

Luke 12:34 – "For where your treasure is, there your heart will be also."

Proverbs 27:19 – "As in water face answereth to face, so the heart of man to man."

HEART CHECK QUESTIONS:

1. How do I live up to being God's treasure?

2. What is a masterpiece? How can I become one?

3. How can I become a reflection of Jesus?

Connecting To The Heart Of God:

What steps can I take to deepen my relationship with Him?

Notes:

Prayer:

Father, teach me how deeply You love me. Remind me daily that I am Your masterpiece and Your great treasure. Why do I feel as if I am unworthy; remind me that if I was the only person on the planet, Jesus would have still died for only me. I am Your special treasure, in Jesus' name. Amen!

Daily Devotional

DATE: _____

REFLECTION OF THE DAY

What do you see when you take a close look at your life? We sometimes deceive ourselves by believing we have a good heart and are doing what is right. If you take the time to search your heart, you will find hidden things that are not a reflection of the Christ whom you serve. Even Jesus went through testing and trials to examine His heart to see if it was right toward God for the fulfillment of His assignment. Do you have a specific heart issue that needs to be dealt with? Allow the Lord to deal with it so He can get you back on track to your destiny.

VERSES OF THE DAY

Psalm 51:7 – "Purge me with hyssop, and I shall be clean; wash me, and I shall be whiter than snow."

Matthew 5:8 – "Blessed are the pure in heart, for they shall see God."

HEART CHECK QUESTIONS:

1. How often do I do self-examinations? What do I find?

2. What methods or steps do I use in my examination?

3. Is there a specific heart issue I need to deal with?

Connecting To The Heart Of God:

What steps can I take to deepen my relationship with Him?

Notes:

Prayer:

Father, help me to see clearly what is in my heart. As I search my heart reveal to me the issues I need to deal with. I desire to be like Jesus, having the right heart, so I can fulfill my assignments. Wash and purge me, in Jesus' name. Amen!

Daily Devotional

DATE: _____

Faithfulness is the foundation for every person who has the heart of a servant. To have the heart of a servant speaks of a person who is faithful to the assignments given to them not only by God but also by men. Do you serve with passion and commitment? Are you faithful to the assignments you have been given? Can you be trusted to follow through? As you answer these questions, examine your heart, and ask God to show you if you truly serve Him with all you have. To experience a deep connection to God, you must search your heart to discover if you truly have the heart to serve Him and to serve others.

VERSES OF THE DAY

John 12:26 – "If any man serve Me, let him follow Me; and where I am, there shall also My servant be: if any man serve Me, him will My Father honour."

Galatians 5:13 – "For, brethren, ye have been called unto liberty; only use not liberty for an occasion to the flesh, but by love serve one another."

HEART CHECK QUESTIONS:

1. Do I serve God and others with passion and faithfulness? How?

2. Can people trust me to follow through on my word?

3. Am I faithful in my relationship with Jesus?

Connecting To The Heart Of God:

What steps can I take to deepen my relationship with Him?

Notes:

Prayer:

Father, thank You for Your faithfulness in my life. Teach me to be a person who follows through on my word at all times. Teach me to have a heart to serve You and Your people. Help me to follow You each day of my life, in Jesus' name. Amen!

Daily Devotional

DATE: _____

REFLECTION OF THE DAY

Our heart is the substance or core of who we are. It is the seat of our desires, emotions, intellect, mind, passion, and wills. What is in our heart motivates and propels us to do things that are in accordance with God's will for our lives or not. God looks at our hearts, and He blesses and promotes us based on what He finds there. Do you have a heart to please Him and to bless the lives of people? When God looks at your heart does He find Himself stamped all over it, or is your heart so crowded with worldly things that a search has to be conducted to see if God is living in any portion of it?

VERSES OF THE DAY

Deuteronomy 6:5 – "And thou shalt love the LORD thy God with all thine heart, and with all thy soul, and with all thy might.."

Mark 12:33 – "And to love Him with all the heart, and with all the understanding, and with all the soul, and with all the strength, and to love His neighbour as Himself, is more than all whole burnt offerings and sacrifices."

HEART CHECK QUESTIONS:

1. What does God see when He looks at my heart?

2. Can people see the presence of God in my life? How?

3. How deeply do I love Jesus ? How do I demonstrate it?

Connecting To The Heart Of God:

What steps can you take to deepen your relationship with Him?

Notes:

Prayer:

Father, help me to have the right motivation. It is my desire to be a reflection of Your Son. Help me to please You in all I do. Deuteronomy 6:5 tells me to love the Lord my God with all my heart. I choose to love You each day, in Jesus' name. Amen!

Daily Devotional

DATE: _____

REFLECTION OF THE DAY

God desires His people to live strong, healthy, and abundant lives. He never leaves people in the broken conditions in which He finds them. He always steps in, and in the midst of a crisis, brings wholeness and healing to all who desire to be well. In order for you and me to have a heart of a servant, we must give ourselves totally over to God. Understand your history with God and know He will do for you all He did for those men and women in the Bible. Let the world know you cannot accomplish a single thing without God's help.

VERSES OF THE DAY

John 13:15-16 – *"For I have given you an example, that ye should do as I have done to you. Verily, verily, I say unto you, The servant is not greater than his lord; neither he that is sent greater than He that sent him."*

Ephesians 6:7-8 – *"With good will doing service, as to the Lord, and not to men: Knowing that whatsoever good thing any man doeth, the same shall he receive of the Lord, whether he be bond or free."*

HEART CHECK QUESTIONS:

1. What broken conditions has Jesus found me in?

2. What has Jesus rescued me from?

3. What things can I accomplish with or without Jesus?

Connecting To The Heart Of God:

What steps can I take to deepen my relationship with Him?

Notes:

Prayer:

Father, I know You desire me to live a healthy and abundant life. Help me to have Your heart to serve people. Thank You for always stepping in during my crisis situations and helping me. I know I cannot do anything with You, in Jesus' name. Amen!

Daily Devotional

DATE: _____

When you make a decision to embrace all the plans of God for your life, be determined and steadfast. Set your face like flint as you race toward your destiny. Don't just stumble into your destiny by accident; pursue God so He can reveal it to you, and when He does, embrace all of it. When you put your hands to the plow, go all the way with Jesus. Do not look backwards. Do not take your eyes off Jesus, because all God has for you is in front and not behind you.

VERSES OF THE DAY

Philippians 3:13-14 – "Brethren, I count not myself to have apprehended: but this one thing I do, forgetting those things which are behind, and reaching forth unto those things which are before, II press toward the mark for the prize of the high calling of God in Christ Jesus.

1 Corinthians 15:58 – "Therefore, my beloved brethren, be ye stedfast, unmoveable, always abounding in the work of the Lord, forasmuch as ye know that your labour is not in vain in the Lord."

HEART CHECK QUESTIONS:

1. How steadfast have I been to accomplish God's plan for me?

2. How do I remain steady when facing oppressions?

3. Am I easily moved because of my circumstances?

Connecting To The Heart Of God:

What steps can I take to deepen my relationship with Him?

Notes:

Prayer:

Father, teach me how to be steadfast in my service to You. Help me to find the plans of God for my life. Help me to find Your specific plans for my future. 1 Corinthians 15:58 reminds me to be steadfast and immovable, in Jesus' name. Amen!

Daily Devotional

DATE: _____

REFLECTION OF THE DAY

Commitment means to follow through on your word, to be steadfast and immovable, and to stay the course no matter how difficult the situation might be. As we examine our lives and our connection to God, we must ask ourselves some questions. Have I been a committed person? Has my heart remained steadfast in the things I have committed to do? Has commitment been the cornerstone of my life? As you meditate on these questions, you will discover what you are most committed to and how passionate you are in following through on your word.

VERSES OF THE DAY

Proverbs 16:3 – "Commit thy works unto the LORD, and thy thoughts shall be established."

1 Kings 8:61 – "Let your heart therefore be wholly true to the Lord our God, walking in his statutes and keeping his commandments, as at this day."

HEART CHECK QUESTIONS:

1. Have I been truly committed to Jesus?

2. Do I have a steadfast heart?

3. What has been the cornerstones of my life?

Connecting To The Heart Of God:

What steps can I take to deepen my relationship with Him?

Notes:

Prayer:

Father, where have I lacked commitment in my life? Forgive me for my lack of commitment and devotion to You. Search my heart and lead me into a deeper commitment to You, Proverbs 16:3 tells me to commit my ways to You and my plans will succeed, in Jesus' name. Amen!

Daily Devotional

DATE: _____

This is God's amazing commitment to each of His children. His commitment caused Him to give His Son's life for us. Jesus' commitment both to God and to us drove Him to lay down His life to redeem us. In turn, our commitment will allow us to lay down our lives for Him and others. Commitment helps us to hold tightly to what has been entrusted to us. It keeps us pressing into the purposes of God and into His promise of eternal life. God's commitment to us, as seen in Romans 8, should spark a response from us. Our response should be a heart that is completely devoted and committed to Him.

VERSES OF THE DAY

Psalm 37:5 – "Commit thy way unto the LORD; trust also in Him; and He shall bring it to pass."

Numbers 30:2 – "If a man vow a vow unto the LORD, or swear an oath to bind his soul with a bond; he shall not break his word, he shall do according to all that proceedeth out of his mouth."

HEART CHECK QUESTIONS:

1. What things have Jesus personally promised me?

2. How has He fulfilled His commitment to me?

3. What things must I do to connect to Jesus?

Connecting To The Heart Of God:

What steps can you take to deepen your relationship with Him?

Notes:

Prayer:

Father, I thank You for Your deep commitment to me. You have demonstrated this commitment by sending, Your Son to die for me. Jesus, thank You for saying 'yes' to saving my life. Psalm 37:5 tells me to commit my ways to You. I commit my ways to You, in Jesus' name. Amen!

Daily Devotional

DATE: _____

REFLECTION OF THE DAY

God first teaches us commitment by demonstrating His commitment to us. He is always with us no matter where we are in our relationship to Him. God released His power, the Holy Spirit, into our lives when we made a commitment to serve and follow Jesus Christ. He gives us power to live lives that are pleasing to Him. He gives us power to glorify His Son. He gives us power to step away from hopelessness and to live in hope. He gives us power to triumph in the midst of difficulties. He gives us power to live lives crowned with integrity. He gives us power to stay the course even when life becomes difficult.

VERSES OF THE DAY

John 14:26 – "But the Helper, the Holy Spirit, whom the Father will send in my name, he will teach you all things and bring to your remembrance all that I have said to you."

1 Corinthians 3:17 – "Now the Lord is the Spirit, and where the Spirit of the Lord is, there is freedom."

HEART CHECK QUESTIONS:

1. What power has God given to me?

2. How can I use God's power for greater things?

3. What is my relationship to the Holy Spirit?

Connecting To The Heart Of God:

What steps can I take to deepen my relationship with Him?

Notes:

Prayer:

Father, thank You for the hope I have is Jesus. Because of His sacrifice I am not without hope. Thank You for the power You have given me to overcome in the midst of all my difficulties, in Jesus' name. Amen!

Daily Devotional

DATE: _____

Some of us have lost our intimate connection to God. As a result, we are not experiencing the blessings, favor, provision, and fullness of life He intends us to have. To reconnect our hearts to God, we must rededicate our lives to Him, so He can saturate us with the wellspring of living water that flows out of His heart toward us. Dedication means to be devoted to the one you love. It is to consecrate yourself, to give all you have to the source of your dedication, to be honorable in your intentions, to be considerate, and to show favor. Our devotion must first be toward God because He has demonstrated His complete devotion toward us.

VERSES OF THE DAY

Joshua 1:8 – "This book of the law shall not depart out of thy mouth; but thou shalt meditate therein day and night, that thou mayest observe to do according to all that is written therein: for then thou shalt make thy way prosperous, and then thou shalt have good success."

Psalm 119:1-3 – "Blessed are the undefiled in the way, who walk in the law of the LORD. Blessed are they that keep His testimonies, and that seek Him with the whole heart. They also do no iniquity: they walk in His ways."

HEART CHECK QUESTIONS:

1. What things have diminished my passion for the things of God?

2. What does it personally mean to me to be crucified with Christ?

3. What is my relationship to the Holy Spirit?

Connecting To The Heart Of God:

What steps can I take to deepen my relationship with Him?

Notes:

Prayer:

Father, teach me how to long after only You. I desire to experience all of Your blessings. How can I rededicate my life to You so I can experience Your fulness of life. Give me a heart of devotion, in Jesus' name. Amen!

Daily Devotional

DATE:_____

REFLECTION OF THE DAY

Our first act of devotion is to move self out of the way, so God can be enthroned in our hearts. We must acknowledge there is One who is greater than we, and He must take center stage in our lives. Through devotion, we allow God to be the only One to live and reign completely in our hearts and lives. His great love for us motivates us to serve Him and to fulfill His plans in the earth. He died for our sins and to free us from shame. In being crucified with Him, we have died to our own plans, our old lifestyles, our will, and a desire to have things our way; we are now committed to what He wants to accomplish through us.

VERSES OF THE DAY

Philippians 4:8 – "Finally, brethren, whatsoever things are true, whatsoever things are honest, whatsoever things are just, whatsoever things are pure, whatsoever things are lovely, whatsoever things are of good report; if there be any virtue, and if there be any praise, think on these things."

Galatians 2:20 - "I am crucified with Christ: nevertheless I live; yet not I, but Christ liveth in me: and the life which I now live in the flesh I live by the faith of the Son of God, who loved me, and gave himself for me."

HEART CHECK QUESTIONS:

1. How much of self sits on the throne of my life?

2. Who has *first* place in my heart?

3. What is my understanding of Jesus' sacrifice for me?

Connecting To The Heart Of God:

What steps can I take to deepen my relationship with Him?

Notes:

Prayer:

Father, I am so thankful that Jesus was willing to die such a horrific death for me. I am truly thankful for His surrender to Your will and plans to redeem us. Philippians 4:8 says to only think on what is pure and lovely. Help me t do this in Jesus' name. Amen!

Daily Devotional

DATE: _____

Once you become dedicated and devoted to the Lord, you will discover you have been equipped with a heart that desires to give. In giving, you demonstrate you are created in the image of the Father, Son, and Holy Spirit, because they are always giving to us. The Father hears and answers us when we pray; the Son shows us compassion and love when we slip and fall from grace; and the Holy Spirit comforts and leads us away from evil and onto paths that honor the Son. God uses our giving to bless and prosper us. The promise in the scripture is that whatever you give will be given back to you, and it will be returned in a greater measure.

VERSES OF THE DAY

Luke 6:38 – "Give, and it shall be given unto you; good measure, pressed down, and shaken together, and running over, shall men give into your bosom. For with the same measure that ye mete withal it shall be measured to you again."

Colossians 3:17 – "And whatever you do in word or deed, do all in the name of the Lord Jesus, giving thanks to God the Father through Him.

HEART CHECK QUESTIONS:

1. How can I be more like Jesus?

2. Am I a giver? How do I demonstrate this?

3. What things am I unwilling to give?

Connecting To The Heart Of God:

What steps can I take to deepen my relationship with Him?

<u>Notes:</u>

Prayer:

Father, I am reminded daily of the fact that God the Father, Son and Holy Spirit are always giving to us. I am a recipient of all His wonderful gifts. Make me more like You, giving of myself, my love, and time to encourage all who I meet, in Jesus' name. Amen!

Daily Devotional

DATE: _____

REFLECTION OF THE DAY

The blessings God give to you will run over because there will not be room enough to handle the abundant supply God will keep pouring out. Some of us may attempt to receive the blessings of the Lord in our hands, but because He always goes above and beyond what we can think or imagine, He has to pour His blessings into our laps. God intends for you to overflow in such a way that your life cannot contain the favor, blessings, provisions, and fullness of joy He has in store for you. When you are devoted to God and have a heart to give what He has given to you, God will make sure that what you receive in return is far greater than what you gave away.

VERSES OF THE DAY

James 1:17 – "Every good gift and every perfect gift is from above, and cometh down from the Father of lights, with whom is no variableness, neither shadow of turning."

2 Corinthians 9:8 – "And God is able to make all grace abound toward you; that ye, always having all sufficiency in all things, may abound to every good work."

HEART CHECK QUESTIONS:

1. Am I currently experiencing God's blessings? How?

2. How do I limit the abundance God wants to give me?

3. What hinders me from receiving God's favor in my life?

Connecting To The Heart Of God:

What steps can I take to deepen my relationship with Him?

<u>Notes:</u>

Prayer:

Father, I need all Your blessings to flood and overtake my life. Help me to receive Your abundant supply each and every day. 2 Corinthians 9:8 says God is able to make all grace abound to me, in Jesus' name. Amen!

Daily Devotional

DATE:_____

REFLECTION OF THE DAY

Dedication and honor go hand in hand; both speak of the intentions of our hearts. To be honorable, we must first understand to whom honor is due. All honor belongs to God because He is El Elyon, the Most High God. As His children, we must glorify Him on a regular basis, because He is worthy of all honor and praise. Our lives must be honorable, our intentions must be honorable, and our motives should be honorable at all times. The Holy Spirit's power in our hearts enables us to be honorable in our dealings with God and with people. He causes us to make decisions that honor God.

VERSES OF THE DAY

1 Samuel 2:30 – "Wherefore the LORD God of Israel saith, I said indeed that thy house, and the house of thy father, should walk before Me for ever: but now the LORD saith, Be it far from Me; for them that honour Me I will honour, and they that despise Me shall be lightly esteemed.

Hebrews 13:18 – "Pray for us: for we trust we have a good conscience, in all things willing to live honestly.

HEART CHECK QUESTIONS:

1. How honorable am I in my relationship with Jesus?

2. How honorable am I in my relationship with others?

3. Do I have a clear conscience?

Connecting To The Heart Of God:

What steps can I take to deepen my relationship with Him?

Notes:

Prayer:

Father, please teach me how to be an honorable person. Where I have shown dishonor to You, I ask for Your forgiveness. Where I have been dishonorable to my loved ones, I ask for Your mercy. Help me to be honorable in all things based on Hebrews 13:18, in Jesus' name. Amen!

Daily Devotional

DATE: _____

REFLECTION OF THE DAY

Consideration requires a deliberate act from each of us. When we are considerate of others, we seek to be a blessing to them. Consideration and dedication will produce a harvest in our lives and in the lives of those who need a helping hand. To be considerate means we say yes whenever a need is presented to us, and we have the ability to fulfill it. Consideration begins in our heart, because it is from our hearts, we esteem others highly and decide to provide for their needs. Not only do we need to be considerate toward people, but we must show consideration to God.

VERSES OF THE DAY

Philippians 2:3-4 - "Let nothing be done through strife or vainglory; but in lowliness of mind let each esteem other better than themselves. Look not every man on his own things, but every man also on the things of others."

Hebrews 10:24-25 – "And let us consider one another to provoke unto love and to good works: Not forsaking the assembling of ourselves together, as the manner of some is; but exhorting one another: and so much the more, as ye see the day approaching."

HEART CHECK QUESTIONS:

1. How considerate am I?

2. What motivates me to be more considerate?

3. How considerate am I in my dealings with God?

Connecting To The Heart Of God:

What steps can I take to deepen my relationship with Him?

Notes:

Prayer:

Father, I recognize that I am not always as considerate as I should be to You and to my loved ones.Teach me to have greater consideration for all the people in my life. Hebrews 10:25 tells me to encourage each other as times are changing all around us, in Jesus' name. Amen!

Daily Devotional

DATE: _____

REFLECTION OF THE DAY

Are you listening to God's instructions for your life and what He wants you to do with your resources? Is it the desire of your heart to please Him? Do you see others in need, yet pass them by even though you have the means to bless them? If your deepest desire is to please God, then first take care of what He has asked you to do and do it without delay. When you obey God and give careful consideration to His needs, God will feed, clothe, dress, and keep you warm. He will take care of every one of your needs—financial, emotional, spiritual, and relational. We must understand God comes first and give consideration to the things that matter to Him.

VERSES OF THE DAY

Psalm 32:8-9 – "I will instruct thee and teach thee in the way which thou shalt go: I will guide thee with Mine eye. Be ye not as the horse, or as the mule, which have no understanding: whose mouth must be held in with bit and bridle, lest they come near unto thee."

Jeremiah 33:3 – "Call unto Me, and I will answer thee, and shew thee great and mighty things, which thou knowest not."

HEART CHECK QUESTIONS:

1. How often do I call upon God for help?

2. Am I considerate with my resources?

3. What blessings come to me when I am considerate?

Connecting To The Heart Of God:

What steps can I take to deepen my relationship with Him?

Notes:

Prayer:

God, please help me to be a more caring and thoughtful person. Help me to care more deeply about You and Your people, in Jesus' name. Amen!

Daily Devotional

DATE: _____

REFLECTION OF THE DAY

Favor enriches our lives because our hearts are confident and secure in the Lord. When we are favored, we have victory in all circumstances and victory over the enemy. As you show favor, God will ensure you are highly favored. When you show favor, it brings a shield of protection to your life. Favor opens doors for you and gives you preferential treatment. Favor will bring promotion and increase to your life, even ahead of people who are more qualified than you are. Favor will bring you an abundance of good things, which will cause you to increase, so you can be a greater blessing in the Kingdom of God.

VERSES OF THE DAY

Luke 2:52 – "And Jesus increased in wisdom and stature, and in favour with God and man.."

Psalm 5:12 – "For thou, LORD, wilt bless the righteous; with favour wilt Thou compass him as with a shield."

HEART CHECK QUESTIONS:

1. Am I experiencing God's favor? How?

2. What doors have opened in my life due to God's favor?

3. How do I gain God's favor?

Connecting To The Heart Of God:

What steps can I take to deepen my relationship with Him?

<u>Notes:</u>

Prayer:

Father, I desire to experience more of Your favor in my life and my family. Favor is better than money. Luke 2:52 says Jesus grew in wisdom and stature and in favor with God first, and then with people. Help me to gain favor with You each day, in Jesus' name. Amen!

Daily Devotional

DATE: _____

REFLECTION OF THE DAY

Trust is a key factor in our relationships not only with God but with others as well. Trust speaks of being dependable, reliable, faithful, believable, credible, and loyal. A trustworthy person understands as they trust God with all their heart, He will pour His goodness and blessings into their life They understand God must be consulted in every decision. They depend on Him and obey His instructions. When God is the center of your life, you will consult Him in every decision, because you understand He can be trusted to lead you down paths that will bring blessings to you and honor to Him.

VERSES OF THE DAY

Isaiah 26:3-4 – "Thou wilt keep him in perfect peace, whose mind is stayed on thee: because he trusteth in thee. Trust ye in the LORD for ever: for in the LORD JEHOVAH is everlasting strength:"

Jeremiah 17:7-8 – "Trust ye in the LORD for ever: for in the LORD JEHOVAH is everlasting strength: For he shall be as a tree planted by the waters, and that spreadeth out her roots by the river, and shall not see when heat cometh, but her leaf shall be green; and shall not be careful in the year of drought, neither shall cease from yielding fruit.

HEART CHECK QUESTIONS:

1. How trusting am I?

2. Do I trust God more than I do others in my life? How?

3. How often do I consult God before making decisions?

Connecting To The Heart Of God:

What steps can I take to deepen my relationship with Him?

Notes:

Prayer:

Father, at times it is hard to trust Your promises for me. There are days when I struggle to trust You even though I know You are trustworthy. I struggle because my circumstances are hard and painful and You have not yet answered me. Please help me to keep trusting You no matter what I face, in Jesus' name. Amen!

Daily Devotional

DATE: _____

To be faithful, you must be filled with faith. This means you have faith in God and in His plans and promises for you. Faithfulness is measured by your willingness to handle the little things in your life as if they were most important. This means you give careful attention to the small things and don't neglect them, even if they seem insignificant to you. Demonstrating faithfulness means you not only talk about it but you live it out day by day. Stephen was not only filled with faith but was faithful in his service to God. Understand, whatever God has assigned you to do, He expects you to be faithful to that assignment.

VERSES OF THE DAY

Proverbs 3:3 – "Let not mercy and truth forsake thee: bind them about thy neck; write them upon the table of thine heart."

1 Samuel 12:24 – "Only fear the LORD, and serve Him in truth with all your heart: for consider how great things he hath done for you.:

HEART CHECK QUESTIONS:

1. What does faithfulness to God means to me?

2. How have I been faithful to the things God asked me to do?

3. What would my closest friends say about my faithfulness?

Connecting To The Heart Of God:

What steps can I take to deepen my relationship with Him?

Notes:

Prayer:

Father, teach me how to be faithful to You and in my service to You. Remind me often of Your faithfulness to me. Help me to be faithful even in the small things. Proverbs 3:3 tells me not to let faithfulness leave me. Help me, in Jesus' name. Amen!

Daily Devotional

DATE:_____

REFLECTION OF THE DAY

Believability goes along with faithfulness. To be believable, you must be a committed believer and be able to persuade others to your way of thinking. You must have total conviction about your beliefs and sell them your ideas. Your assurance and certainty about what you believe makes you credible. In order for you and me to attain this level of believability, we must be filled with the wisdom and the knowledge of God.

VERSES OF THE DAY

Hebrews 11:6 – "But without faith it is impossible to please Him: for he that cometh to God must believe that He is, and that He is a rewarder of them that diligently seek Him."

Mark 9:23 – "Jesus said unto him, If thou canst believe, all things are possible to him that believeth."

HEART CHECK QUESTIONS:

1. What is the foundation of my belief?

2. What is my level of conviction about Jesus?

3. Am I a credible person? State examples.

Connecting To The Heart Of God:

What steps can I take to deepen my relationship with Him?

<u>Notes:</u>

Prayer:

Father, I have not always been firm in my belief about You and to share those beliefs with others. Help me to be totally convinced that You died in my place. Give me credibility with people. In Mark 9:23, Jesus tells us all things are possible to those who believe, in Jesus' name. Amen!

Daily Devotional

DATE: _____

REFLECTION OF THE DAY

We must become credible witnesses for our King. We must also be authentic in our faith and dependable in our service to God. A credible person is both trustworthy and reliable. A credible person does not put their hope in worldly things but in God who is the supplier of all things. Timothy gives a warning to those who are rich to watch their attitude, because wealth can be unreliable and does not bring credibility. He warns us not to be proud because we are financially blessed, but to use these blessings to help those in need. God gives us wealth to fulfill His purposes in the earth.

VERSES OF THE DAY

Proverbs 10:9 – "He that walketh uprightly walketh surely: but he that perverteth his ways shall be known."

John 16:13 – "Howbeit when He, the Spirit of truth, is come, He will guide you into all truth: for He shall not speak of Himself; but whatsoever He shall hear, that shall He speak: and He will shew you things to come."

HEART CHECK QUESTIONS:

1. How authentic am I about my faith?

2. Have I been trustworthy before God and others?

3. Is my life crowned with integrity?

Connecting To The Heart Of God:

What steps can I take to deepen my relationship with Him?

<u>Notes:</u>

Prayer:

Father, I am striving each day to be a credible person. Make me a trustworthy and faithful person. Father, You are filled with integrity, and is my perfect example of all things that are good. Proverbs 10:9 says when I walk with integrity I walk safely. Teach me how to walk with You each day, in Jesus' name. Amen!

Daily Devotional

DATE: _____

REFLECTION OF THE DAY

A loyal person is dedicated to what they believe. They are faithful, committed, true to who they are, and devoted to their cause. A person who is loyal reflects the attributes of God. God is loyal and faithful to us even when we are unfaithful to Him. His love and His compassion are constant and unchanging. You can never commit a sin so great that it will change God's love and faithfulness toward you. This is why a person who may be sitting on death row can repent of his or her sins, and God will instantly forgive and provide them with eternal life. He is loyal, faithful, and steadfast in His devotion to His children.

VERSES OF THE DAY

Deuteronomy 7:9 – "Know therefore that the LORD thy God, He is God, the faithful God, which keepeth covenant and mercy with them that love Him and keep His commandments to a thousand generations;

Titus 2:7 – "In all things shewing thyself a pattern of good works: in doctrine shewing uncorruptness, gravity, sincerity,"

HEART CHECK QUESTIONS:

1. What do I know about God's nature?

2. How often do I look like Jesus? Give examples.

3. Do those who know me say I am loyal? Site example.

Connecting To The Heart Of God:

What steps can I take to deepen my relationship with Him?

Notes:

Prayer:

Father, I am thankful for Your love and faithfulness to me even in the hard seasons of my life. Thank You for Your love and constant compassion over the years. I am thankful to You for Jesus. Help me to be more like Him each day, in Jesus' name. Amen!

Daily Devotional

DATE: _____

REFLECTION OF THE DAY

To talk about humility is to talk about the life of Jesus and the example He has given to us. Jesus vividly modeled humility for us. He who is equal with God laid aside His glory and splendor, thus shedding His divine nature, to be born of a woman so He could redeem us. What Jesus did is humility in its deepest form. Jesus emptied Himself of His heavenly status and temporarily relinquished His power, while letting go of all His heavenly worship, so He could take on the form of a servant in order to save us.

VERSES OF THE DAY

Philippians 2:8 – "And being found in fashion as a man, He humbled Himself, and became obedient unto death, even the death of the cross."

Colossians 3:12 - "Put on therefore, as the elect of God, holy and beloved, bowels of mercies, kindness, humbleness of mind, meekness, longsuffering;Put on then, as God's chosen ones, holy and beloved, compassionate hearts, kindness, humility, meekness, and patience."

HEART CHECK QUESTIONS:

1. What have I laid aside to pursue Jesus?

2. How do I define humility?

3. In what ways do I operate in humility?

Connecting To The Heart Of God:

What steps can I take to deepen my relationship with Him?

Notes:

Prayer:

Father, I am so grateful for Jesus' humility. Because of His humility, He went to the cross to die for me. Teach me how to be clothed with humility so I can be like Jesus! Philippians 2:8 reminds me Jesus humbled Himself. Help me to humble-myself, in Jesus' name. Amen!

Daily Devotional

DATE:_____

When we acknowledge we can do nothing in our own strength and power, God will begin to dispense His love and humility through each of us. The humility we show to one another will be the proof that our humility before God is real and genuine. True humility is not demonstrated in how we pray or in our daily devotional with God, but in how we live each day to glorify and honor Him. How humble are you in your unguarded moments when no one is looking? Humility is the proof of our righteousness. We demonstrate through humility we have right standing with God.

VERSES OF THE DAY

1 John 4:20 – "If a man say, I love God, and hateth his brother, he is a liar: for he that loveth not his brother whom he hath seen, how can he love God whom he hath not seen?"

2 Chronicles 7:14 – "If my people, which are called by My name, shall humble themselves, and pray, and seek My face, and turn from their wicked ways; then will I hear from heaven, and will forgive their sin, and will heal their land."

HEART CHECK QUESTIONS:

1. How do I daily glorify God?

2. How can I model the humility of Jesus?

3. How can I get God to answer my prayers requests?

Connecting To The Heart Of God:

What steps can I take to deepen my relationship with Him?

Notes:

Prayer:

Father, teach me how to live each day to glorify Jesus. Remind me that you are always aware of my actions and to be humble in my unguarded moments. Help me to be like YOU in every way, in Jesus' name. Amen!

List All Your Prayers That God Has Answered!

NOTES:

Prayer for Wisdom and Favor

Father, I (your name) seek You for wisdom in all areas of my life. Proverbs 8:33-35 says that I should listen to instructions and be wise and that if I listen to wisdom, I will be happy because wisdom will be watching at my doors each day. Thank You that when I find wisdom, I find life and obtain favor from the Lord. Father, Proverbs 8:1 says that wisdom calls out to me and that wisdom is better than precious stones and nothing desirable can compare with her. It says, "I, wisdom, share a home with shrewdness and have knowledge and discretion." I ask You, Father, to help me share my heart with wisdom.

Father, I thank You that John 14:14 says that if I ask anything in Your name You will do it, so I ask You today to fill me with wisdom in every decision I make, in Jesus' name. I thank You, Lord, that Proverbs 16:3 says for me to commit my ways to You, and all my plans will succeed. Father, Psalm 50:15 says that when I call to You in the day of trouble, You will rescue me, and You will honor me. I call to You today and ask You to fill me with wisdom and to rescue me from all fiery trials, in Jesus' name.

Author, Joan E. Murray I MUST PRAY

Prayer for Integrity in My Life

Father, in the name of Jesus, I ask You to fulfill my desire to help others and be a blessing to them. Mark 4:24 says that if I pay attention to what I hear, everything will be measured and added to my life. Father, just as Abraham believed You and it was credited to him for righteousness, so Galatians 3:6 says You credit me with the ability through Your righteousness to provide aid to others when You present their needs to me. Your Word promises in Psalm 84:11 that You will give me grace and glory and that You do not withhold anything good from those who live in integrity. Proverbs 28:18 says whoever walks in integrity will be delivered, but he who is crooked in his ways will suddenly fall. Proverbs 2:20-21 also says that by Your wisdom, discretion, and understanding, we will walk in the way of the good and keep to the paths of the righteous; for the upright will inhabit the land, and those with integrity will remain in it.

Thank you that I am a person of integrity who will do for others what You have instructed me to do. I thank You that You have taught me to live like Philippians 4:11, being content in whatever circumstance I find myself. I thank You that Colossians 3:23 says that whatever I do, to do it enthusiastically as something done for the Lord and not men. Help me to be enthusiastic about helping others find their position in You. I thank You Father, that Psalm 102:13 says that You will arise and have compassion on Zion (your name) for it is time to show favor to her, the appointed time has come. I stand in the place of Zion, and I take this promise for my life and loved ones. I thank You that Your favor and integrity will begin to abound in my life and flood and overtake me, in Jesus' name.

Author, Joan E. Murray, I MUST PRAY

**If you would like to know more about
Joan Murray Ministries,
please contact us at:**

**Joan Murray Ministries
P.O. Box 5073
Katy, TX 77491
281-398-2501**

**E-Mail: jmmcontactus@gmail.com
www.joanmurrayministries.org**

**Changing Lives Through the Power and
Truth of God's Word.**

www.ingramcontent.com/pod-product-compliance
Lightning Source LLC
Chambersburg PA
CBHW070939120626

46546CB00004B/1485